Foreword

I am delighted to have been asked to write the foreword to this book. It gives me the chance to acknowledge this innovative series of books created with, and for young carers by Sefton Carers Centre.

Although I consider myself lucky to have been highly successful in business, I have never forgotten my roots. Growing up I went to nine different schools and lived in nine different houses, many of which were in what today would be called disadvantaged areas of Liverpool. That upbringing certainly helped both shape me as a person and prepare me for my business life to come.

Having supported many charities on a personal level throughout my Redrow career, in 2001 I started the Foundation because I wanted to give back to society. I wanted to make a difference to the lives of people in the areas I was born and raised.

Most of all I want to help people coping with disability and disadvantage by supporting local charities that are doing practical things to help people; charities which have a real impact at the grass roots of society. Sefton Carers Centre is one such charity; the Foundation is pleased to be supporting the Young Carers Service.

Carers of all ages face many issues and challenges throughout their own lives and that of the person they care for. Young carers rarely see themselves as carers and don't often recognise the importance of their own lives and happiness. These books will enable young carers to identify with the central character, their day to day reality and the impact support can bring, whilst offering uplifting stories that are an inspiration to all.

The books are a fictional interpretation of the young carers stories, showing the super-human effort some young carers go through each day and also the difference the support, care and comradeship offered to young carers by the young carers project, professionals, schools, friends and family can make.

I hope that young carers will enjoy these books, seeing themselves in the central role and how with support they can continue caring with the confidence they are not alone.

Steve Morgan CBE
Founder and Chairman, Steve Morgan Foundation

WITH A CARE
IN
THE WORLD

A Young Carer's story of caring for
someone with Mental Health Problems

By Charles Lea
Illustrated by Andrew Mulvenna

A Note from Sefton Carers

Grace is a fictional young carer, but her story has been based on the real-life experiences of young carers who live in Sefton. Over Autumn 2019 author Charles Lea met with a number of these amazing young people and listened to what they had to say about their lives. From these accounts he wrote this story and three other stories about young carers who look after members of their family.

A Carer is anyone who helps look after someone in their family who is ill or has a disability. Sefton Carers Centre is a local charity who will listen and provide support to any carer who is over the age of 5.

There are many children out there, not only in Sefton, but throughout the United Kingdom and the world who care for their families and do not know of the support which Sefton Carers Centre, and other organisations, can give to them.

We hope all four of these stories show you just how young carers can be helped, as they, themselves, help others.

The other stories in the "With A Care in the World" collection are:

Evie   A young carer's story of caring for someone with Autism

Anya   A young carer's story of caring for someone with Dementia

Rishi   A young carer's story of caring for someone with Cancer.

If you, a family member or friend, need help and support as a young carer you can contact Sefton Young Carers Team on 0151 288 6060 or e-mail help@carers.sefton.gov.uk. Information about Sefton Young Carers Service can also be found on website www.sefton-carers.org.uk.

"With A Care in the World. Grace, a young carer's story of caring for someone with Mental Health Problems" first published 2020 by Sefton Carers Centre, 27 to 37 South Road, Waterloo, L22 5PE. Sefton Carers Centre is a registered charity in England and Wales, No: 1050808. Registered as a company limited by guarantee in England No: 3124430.

The right of Charles Lea to be identified as the author of this work has been asserted by him.

The right of Andrew Mulvenna to be identified as the illustrator of this work has been asserted by him.

ISBN Number 978-1-9163406-1-9

Cover Design by Suzanne Green. Layout and Typeset by Rob Russell.

Grace's Story

I love days out to Formby nature reserve.

We don't go there that often, so it always makes it special when we do.

I love the changing scenes from the beautiful woodlands and then through onto the beach and the sea. Sometimes, in the woods, the bushes are all tightly packed around you and the trees cover the sky and it can feel like you are fenced in a bit but then you reach gaps in the woods, where you can see the sky and have more room to run around in and breathe.

From there you can run up and fall down the sand dunes and then onto the beach itself, warm, sunny and golden in the summer; cold, exposed and lonely in the winter.

You cannot go to Formby without seeing the red squirrels that live there but, for me, I love to see the horses, all the horses, hacking along paths in the woods and then galloping at high speed on the sand.

One day I hope to have a horse. They are my favourite everything, way more intelligent and loving than some of us humans. Riding along on the beach, they, and their riders, seem free, free and fast, to go wherever they want to in the whole world.

And I know all about looking after horses too. Sometimes, not as often as I would like, I help at a stable not very far from where I live. One of the owners will even let me ride her old horse, Taz, if I do all the other things too, things like mucking out, give Taz some water and hay and then sweep the floor of the stables clean. Its hard work but I love it, especially when I can ride him in the field or on a hack around our local area. This is when I feel free myself.

Who knows, perhaps one day I could ride a horse at Aintree Racecourse, perhaps even win the Grand National.

I would love to have Taz come home with me, but I don't think he would quite fit in at our house. Anyway, I have enough on my plate already.

Let me explain why.

Whoops, before I do, let me introduce myself to you. My name is Grace and I am nine years old. I live with my Mum and my two twin sisters, Poppy and Autumn who are five years old.

Some people might say that we are not that typical a family. But I would not know any different and, besides, this is my family and I am proud to be a part of it.

But we do have our problems. You see my Mum suffers from depression which means she feels down and upset pretty much all the time. Sometimes she will have a drink to help her feel better. I don't mean have a cup of tea by the way. I mean she drinks booze, sometimes in the day.

When I found out that she was depressed it was really upsetting to know that my lovely Mum felt so low. I had to step in and play mum for the twins and do everything for them: wash; put to bed; cook tea, really everything a parent does.

I have tried to not let it change my life, but it hasn't been easy. Like, for example, some days after coming home from school I want to go and play with my friends or go with a couple of them and look after Taz but if my Mum is drinking I have to help with the twins and get them fed and get them to bed.

It hasn't really affected my relationship with my real friends because they understand but I do miss them quite a lot, especially when they go to the stables. When I see them the next day in school I always ask what they did with Taz and where did they ride him and what sort of mood was he in as he can be playful one minute and then cheeky the next.

My twin sisters are like Taz, cheeky and playful but I can see that they feel sadness too, because of Mum. They want to come home from school and give her a big cuddle and tell her what has been going on in school, who said what, who got told off and what nice things their teacher said about them.

I can't stop them doing this and I know my Mum loves it when they come back but then, a second later, it becomes a bit too much for her as the twins can become hyper, so she goes into her room and stays there. I take over then and play with the girls and make them a bit of a snack and put the telly on.

Thing is, I also want to give my mum a big cuddle and tell her everything that went on in school or how I am feeling about things. But I don't, as I don't want my Mum to worry or feel any sadder.

Mum says that drinking can be her medicine as it makes her feel good for a bit. But sometimes, the next day, she is far too hungover to get up and get us all ready for school so I do it and we are often late. I've shouted at my little sisters before and made them cry but I regretted doing that straight away and now I don't. They are only five years old; they don't do things like taking ages to get ready on purpose. They are tired too.

Mum's energy isn't that good either. By the time we get home she is exhausted. She does try to make us some tea but most of the time she does not. Instead we cook something dead easy in the microwave like noodles. She doesn't really eat much herself, so I guess she thinks we don't eat much either.

I've got news for you; the twins could win Olympic Gold for eating if they could. But they don't, thank God, as I stop them. They sometimes complain but I tell them that I will feed them sprouts and cabbage and beans, all in a horse's nosebag and that stops them for a bit.

If Mum isn't drinking her mood can get worse too. She can sometimes go for a few days without any booze and I so wish she would stop forever but everything gets too much for her and she can become all frightened and worried and then, to stop us all seeing her like this, she just goes into her bedroom and hides.

I will make her some food, just in case she wants it but nine times out of ten, it will be left, uneaten.

Once tea is finished I do the cleaning, I can't wait for the twins to get a bit older so they can help too. They can start cleaning the bathroom and especially the toilet! But, for now, it is down to me. I always start in the kitchen, washing up all the dishes and then wiping everywhere before dusting and hoovering the lounge and hall.

Then it's up the stairs and a quick tidy of the twins' room and finally, the bathroom. I think I start downstairs and make my way upstairs so I can just fall onto my bed and lie down for a bit. But, by then, it's only about 7pm, too early for me but the right time to start getting the twins off.

Every other night I like to give them a bath. They love a bath so it is a great way of getting them upstairs but it can never be quick and I have to watch them at all times and, by the time they are out, dry and in bed, they are almost fast asleep before I can read them a story.

Finally, I will put a wash on, ready to hang out in the morning. I don't want us to smell in school and get other children laughing at us. But, to be honest, I don't really care what they think.

I just want Mum to be proud of me when she comes out of her room and think that we can manage.

Well, sort of.

Problems at School

Truth is I am always tired and come the afternoon in school I am like a zombie. I try my best but things like maths and science frazzle my brain. One day my teacher, Mrs Boothman, taught us something called a "delta" in geography. It's kind of like an island but when she asked me what it was, I did not have a clue. When I answered that Delta is a local taxi firm the whole class began laughing.

She thought I was joking but I wasn't, honest.

But there were certainly no jokes to be had with my last report. Mrs Boothman said she would like to speak to my Mum about me as my work was really going downhill and that school had sent a letter to Mum about coming in to discuss this and the fact that me and the twins were late a lot.

At around the same time, something else happened in school. Now most of the other kids are really nice but there are two, sometimes three who can be really cruel. They pick on me not because Mum has mental health problems but because they have heard she likes to drink lots of alcohol.

It started when they would whisper "boozer," to me as I walked past in the corridor or in the playground. Then it became louder and became "boozer loser," and they would chant it across the playground at me and get some others to join in too.

I tried to ignore it and just stay with my real friends, the ones who also go to the stables and look after Taz and other horses but then it got worse. One morning, as we were all walking down the main school corridor I thought they were going to attack me. "Boozer loser, boozer loser," they shouted and the three of them circled me right round.

When I tried to push past to get away one of girls thought I was attacking them back and tried to hit me.

She missed, thankfully, but everyone around us was screaming and a second later two of the teachers arrived and split us all up.

I had to go to the Headteacher and explain my side of what happened. The other three said that I had started it and when I heard that I just burst into tears.

I had never told school about Mum. Mum said it was best not to in case people came around and started to poke into our lives.

But I told my Headteacher everything, about what the bullies had called me, about Mum and her condition and about what I did at home and why we was late sometimes in getting to school and that I was so shattered all the time.

You know, it wasn't nice but afterwards I felt glad I had said it to someone. She believed me too, about the fight in the corridor, and that she wanted to reach out to Mum and help us. I wasn't sure about this at first, but she said it would help Mum and me and my sisters.

Back at Home

The twins have never had a proper birthday party before. They've been to a couple of their friend's parties and we are lucky that other parents will help pick up and bring them home.

One day, whilst they were in the bath, they asked if they could have a birthday party at some soft play centre – I was too tired to remember the name.

This is going to cause a problem and I don't really know what to do.

I know Mum will not want to organise something, its not just the money, and I hear that birthday parties can cost a lot of money, but she doesn't like meeting up with people. It's not just the parents of the other kids, it's even our family. She doesn't like her sisters, or even her Mum, coming around and seeing exactly what she is like. Mum says they will try and split us up and she doesn't want that to happen. I don't too.

Mum says that the idea of her family and organising a party makes her feel more stressed which means she will want more of her medicine.

You know, reading my story back to myself, I have to say she is not that bad. She's not always in her room and I know that her depression is not her fault. She loves us three and says she doesn't want us to be split up or anything like that.

Another thing with the twins birthday though is that I've not really had a proper birthday party with my friends either, so I have no idea what to really do.

It's hard enough to have friends come around for a bit. I don't have time on most school nights to go and see them.

If anything, the only time I get to see them is at the weekend and that is usually at the stables when I can see my handsome Taz.

When school got in contact with Mum about me and my work and being late and all that, she panicked for a bit. As I have said, she doesn't like people being nosy about our family, but two members of staff came out for a home visit and it turned out to be okay, and Mum was happy when I got home. Mum then had a meeting with a counsellor about helping her out too.

As a result of that meeting, I met with this lovely woman called Eve from Sefton Carers.

We spoke, just the two of us, for ages. I told her what I had told my Headteacher and I told her about the bullies too. Again, it was so good to speak to someone and tell them how I feel about things. Eve just listened to me at first and then told me that I wasn't alone.

She told me that there were lots of people like me, and that we were "young carers" and that we were very special. I said I didn't feel special and that anyone would do what I do at home if they were in my shoes.

Eve told me that although it was my Mum who was ill, I also needed help too and that is what she and the rest of the team at Sefton Carers were all about.

A week or so later I went to a youth club at their base in Waterloo and I met a whole load of children, similar in age to me, who all were young carers too. I was amazed at how many children there were. I was a bit shy at first, but Eve introduced me to another new girl called Ella and we chatted about stuff like horses, music and our fave K-Pop bands and it was good.

Now I really look forward to going to youth club and we have all been out to the local cinema, which was an amazing night.

People from Sefton Carers come around to our house to see how we are and discuss any problems we have. They cannot wish away our problems like magic, but they can talk and encourage me and make me feel more upbeat.

I still do all the things for my Mum and the twins. I still get tired at school, but school are really sound with me now and I can go and speak to the Headteacher or the deputy head about things.

Knowing that there is help about and that I am not the only person to be a young carer has made me feel much better. I wish no-one had to care for someone else, but I am happy and proud to look after my lovely Mum.

I have still got the twins birthday to sort out but for my birthday I am going to have the best treat. You see Eve and the other staff at Sefton Carers all love horses too and they found some money for me to have a day out horse riding, at Formby Beach.

I am so excited and cannot wait. I want to groom the horse before we go out and spend some time with him so we can get to know each other. And then! We will be off riding along the gorgeous beach around Formby, just me and my horse. I know it isn't Taz, but he won't mind, he gets so much love already from me and my friends.

I can almost dream it, riding along the enormous beach, a canter here, a gallop there, the wind in my face and feeling free and fast, as if I can ride to the ends of the world, as if I can do anything.

A Note from Sefton Carers and Charles Lea

Many people helped us write this story. Without their support, advice and time we would simply not have been able to have written this story in a way to reflect the true experiences of young carers.

We thank the following for their help:

Greenbank High School Young Carers Group

Holy Family High School Young Carers Group

Sefton Young Carers North & South Youth Clubs

Steve Morgan Foundation

Mersey Care

Sefton MBC

Clatterbridge Cancer Centre

Sefton Library Service